NATIONAL GEOGRAPHIC

Ladders

THE OLD WEST

T0288480

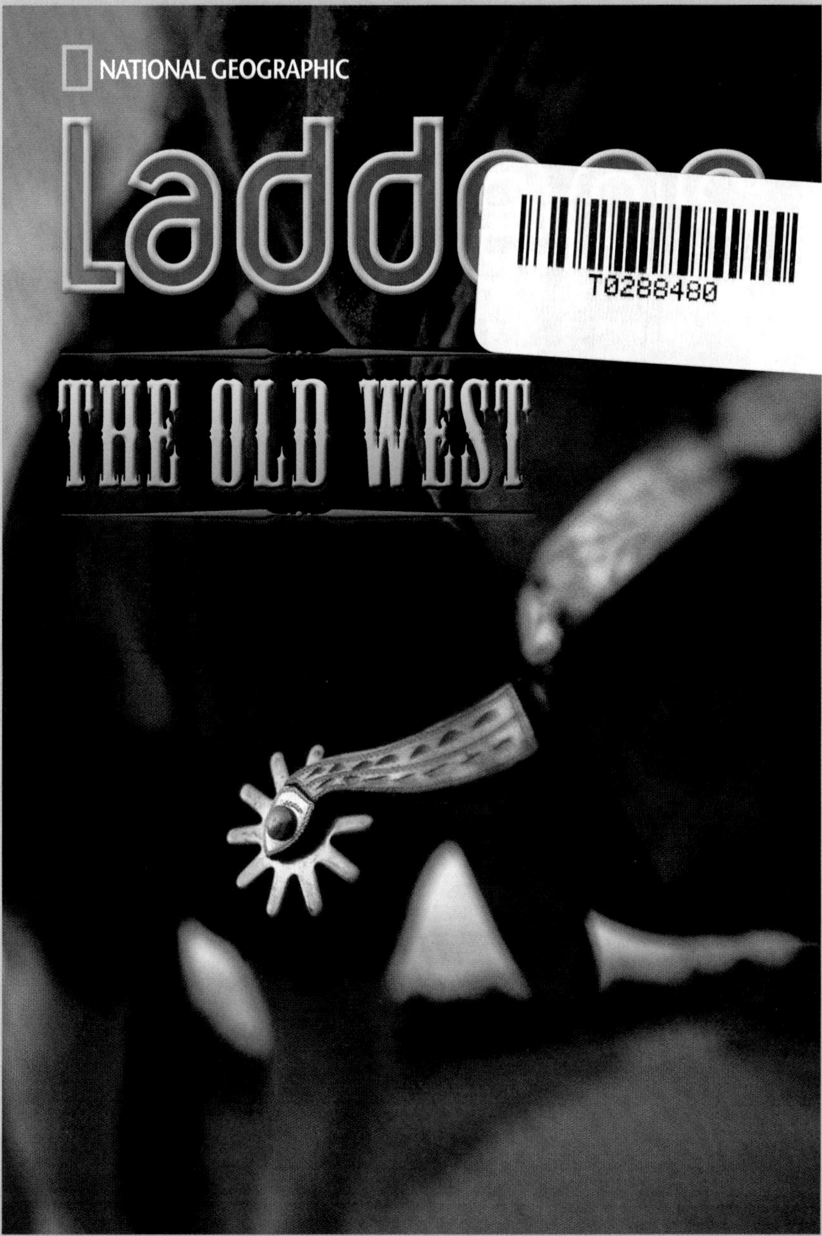

GENRE Song

Read to find out about how the open range inspired poetry.

HOME ON THE RANGE

inspired by the poem "My Western Home" by Dr. Brewster Higley

In 1871, Dr. Brewster Higley left the eastern United States and moved to Kansas. He built a rustic cabin on his own plot of open land. The views surrounding the cabin inspired him to write a poem, and later the poem became a song. The original song was so popular many versions followed. Today we know the song by the title "Home on the Range." The lyrics below come from one of the most familiar versions of the song.

Oh, give me a home, where the buffalo roam
Where the deer and the ***antelope*** *play;*
Where seldom is heard a discouraging word,
And the skies are not cloudy all day.

(Refrain) Home, home on the ***range***
Where the deer and the antelope play;
Where seldom is heard a discouraging word,
And the skies are not cloudy all day.

Where the air is so pure, the zephyrs so free,*
The breezes so balmy and light,
That I would not exchange my home on the range
For all the cities so bright.

(Refrain)

How often at night when the heavens are bright
With the light of the glittering stars,
Have I stood here amazed and asked as I gazed
If their glory exceeds that of ours.

(Refrain)

Oh, I love the wild flowers in this dear land of ours;
The curlew* I love to hear scream;
And I love the white rocks and the antelope flocks,
That graze on the mountain-tops green.

(Refrain)

Oh, give me a land where the bright diamond sand
Flows leisurely down the stream;
Where the graceful white swan goes gliding along
Like a maid in a heavenly dream.

(Refrain)

Then I would not exchange my home on the range,
Where the deer and the antelope play;
Where seldom is heard a discouraging word
And the skies are not cloudy all day.

(Refrain)

* curlew — a large shorebird with brown coloring that breeds in the Great Plains and has a long, curved bill

* zephyr — a gentle breeze that blows from the west

Check In How does the song convey details about the west?

Read to find out about the cowboys of the American Old West.

Cowboy History

by Dennis Fertig

Interstate highways stretch across the broad western United States. Every now and then drivers or passengers will spy something in the dusty distance. "Can that be a cowboy?" they ask themselves in surprise.

Well, yes it might be. Cowboys aren't just legendary figures of the past. Real working cowboys still ride horses and patrol broad ranches to tend cattle—sometimes stubborn, ornery cattle. As they work, these modern cowboys see the cement highways in the distance, but they also see something else: They see the long, proud tradition that they honor in their work. They wear, ride, and carry in their hearts the cowboy way that has lasted for centuries.

What was once considered "The West" included states west of the Mississippi River, Mexico, and part of western Canada.

What Is a Cowboy?

Throughout history, people have herded large groups of animals such as sheep, goats, and pigs. A cowboy is a herder who cares for cattle. Although animal herding might sound simple, being a cowboy has always been hard, challenging, and risky work.

The cowboy tradition started long before there was a country called the United States. In the 1500s, soldiers and settlers from Spain brought two valuable animals to North America: cattle and horses. Native Americans had never seen these large, strange-looking, four-legged beasts before. Eventually though, many Native American people became expert horsemen.

Cattle Ranching and *Vaqueros*

In Mexico and other areas where the Spanish settled, cattle ranching became common. Cattle are prized animals. Cows provide milk that humans drink and also use to make cheese and butter. Cattle are also a source of meat, including steak and hamburger meat. Leather is made from the hides of cattle. In the old days, soap and candles were made from cattle fat, and dried cattle dung was even used as fuel.

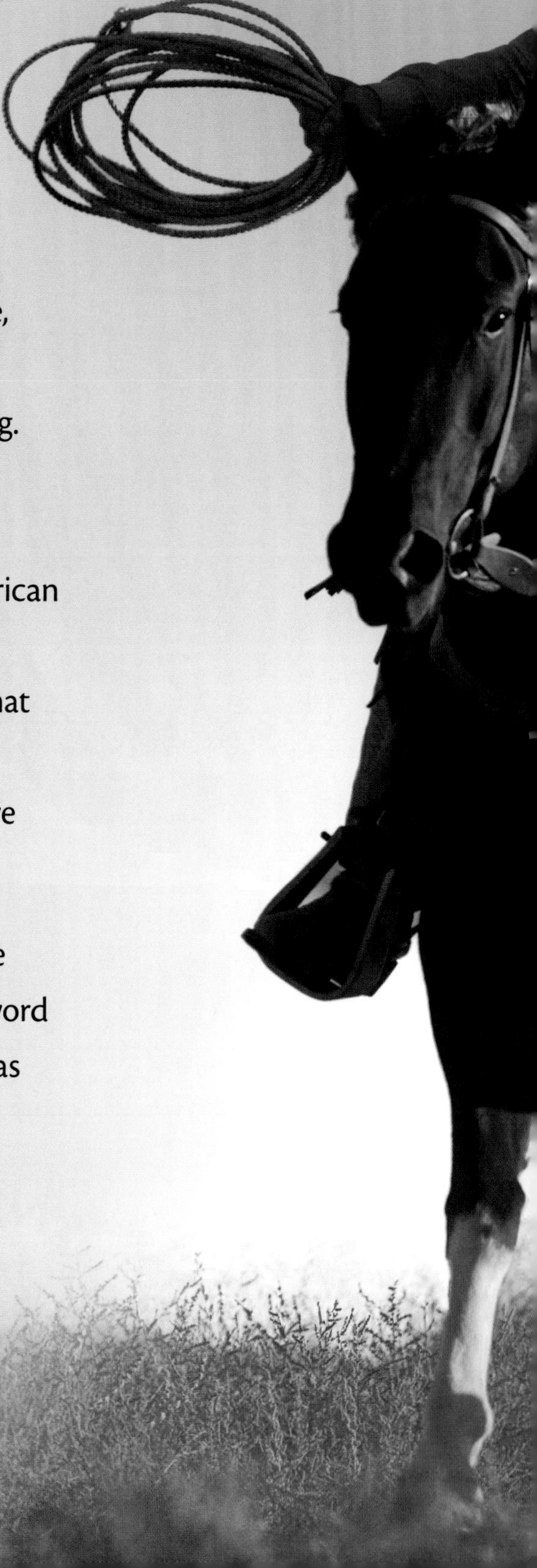

Cattle usually live in herds, and Mexico had large, open areas for those herds to roam. Wealthy Spaniards knew the land was perfect for ranching. *Vaqueros* were horsemen who worked for the wealthy ranchers. *Vaquero* means "cowman" in Spanish, and *vaqueros* were the first North American cowboys. They developed the horse- and cattle-handling techniques, clothing, and equipment that cowboys of the American West eventually used. Some of those first cowboys were enslaved Native Americans forced to work on Spanish ranches.

Many English words about aspects of cowboy life come from Spanish words. One example is the word *buckaroo,* a word that along with *cowpuncher* was commonly used instead of cowboy. *Buckaroo* was how Americans who couldn't speak Spanish tried to pronounce *vaquero.* The Spanish word for *wild* or *stray* was *mesteño.* Today we call wild horses mustangs.

Cowboy Territory

Unique cowboy styles and names developed in different regions of the West.

The open **ranges** of the American West, particularly in Texas, became home to many mustangs. Cowboys caught and broke the wild horses, and the mustang became the cowboy's preferred horse to ride. As American settlers moved to Texas, some took up cattle ranching. Many new Texans, both ranchers and cowboys, learned how to handle cattle and horses from Mexican *vaqueros*.

Roundups and Cattle Drives

Until the Civil War started in 1861, cattle ranching thrived in Texas. The war slowed ranching, and as a result the wild roaming herds of cattle grew larger. After the war, American **expansion** into the West began again and with it cattle ranching resumed, making job opportunities for cowboys plentiful.

Ranchers were the land and cattle owners, but cowboys were the heart of cattle ranches, and ranchers relied heavily on the cowboys who lived and worked on the ranches. The cowboys were responsible for keeping cattle healthy and safe. They also protected the herd from rustlers, thieves who stole cattle.

There are many cattle breeds, but the most common in The Old West was the longhorn. Cowboys of The Old West became skilled in handling this breed. Longhorn cattle were a mixture of the breed the Spanish brought to America and an English breed from the eastern United States. Although longhorns were strong, stubborn, and had dangerous horns, these hard-to-handle animals also could travel long distances living on small amounts of grass and water found in dry western lands.

Ranchers allowed their cattle to mix with other owners' cattle. Cattle had brands, or symbols, that cowboys burnt into cattle's hides with an iron tool. The brands showed which ranchers owned the cattle. Twice a year, roundups occurred and cowboys herded cattle together and sorted them out by brand. Unbranded calves were claimed and branded during the roundup. Cattle could be rounded up and led to distant towns on train lines. The cattle were sold and shipped by train to eastern cities. These long trips from ranges to railroads were called cattle drives. By 1867, cattle drives were becoming common, and the great era of the cowboy had begun. At this time, about a third of the American cowboys were African American or Hispanic, and many cowboys had fought in the Civil War.

The Tools of the Cowboy

Almost everything a cowboy wore or carried was needed for his job.

Horse

The horse, a cowboy's most important tool, was trained to aid in rounding up and controlling longhorns. Smart horses became "cutting horses" that helped a cowboy capture and brand longhorns. Longhorns didn't want to be caught, so the horse and cowboy had to work together quickly and skillfully.

Clothing

Most cowboy clothing was similar to clothing that Mexican cowboys wore.

Cowboys wore a scarf called a bandanna. Dipped in water and wrapped around his neck or under his hat, a bandanna cooled a cowboy off. Worn around his face, it protected him from breathing trail dust. Most of the time, a bandanna just kept dust and dirt outside of a cowboy's shirt.

Clothing, such as shirts, pants, and vests were usually made of a long-lasting flannel material that absorbed sweat and didn't show dirt. They needed durable clothing for protection from the weather and the rigors of their work.

Saddle

Cowboys sat on saddles for long hours, often from sunrise to sundown, so a saddle had to be comfortable. The high back of a saddle helped the cowboy stay put. The front of a saddle had a knob called a horn. It didn't beep but was used to wrap a rope around. Hanging from the saddle were stirrups for a cowboy's feet. Under the stirrups were fenders, pieces of leather that kept the horse's sweat away from the cowboy.

Spurs

Cowboys wore spurs around the ankles of their boots. Spurs were poked into the side of the horse to turn it in the proper direction. The spurs were dull but could get through thick horsehair.

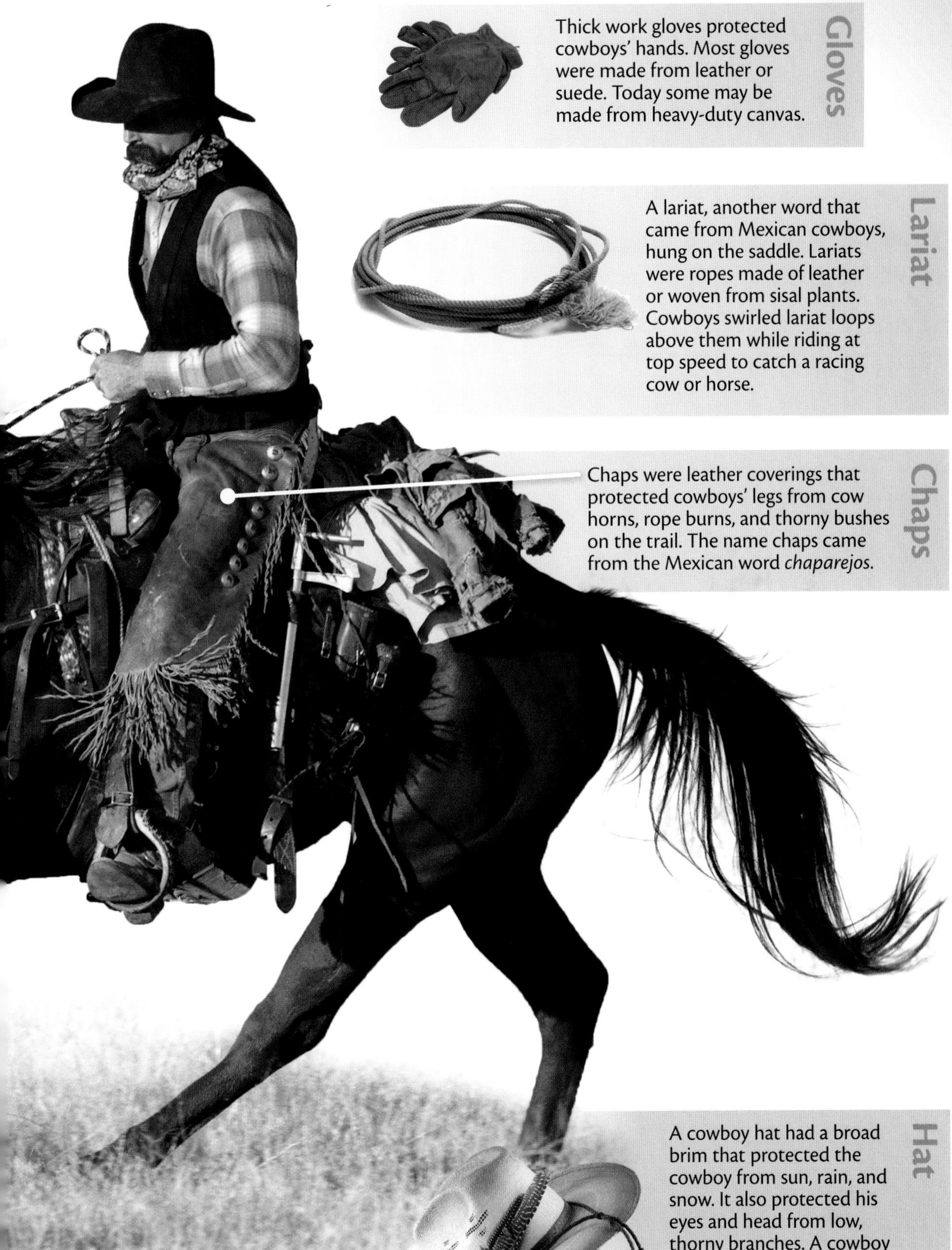

Gloves

Thick work gloves protected cowboys' hands. Most gloves were made from leather or suede. Today some may be made from heavy-duty canvas.

Lariat

A lariat, another word that came from Mexican cowboys, hung on the saddle. Lariats were ropes made of leather or woven from sisal plants. Cowboys swirled lariat loops above them while riding at top speed to catch a racing cow or horse.

Chaps

Chaps were leather coverings that protected cowboys' legs from cow horns, rope burns, and thorny bushes on the trail. The name chaps came from the Mexican word *chaparejos*.

Hat

A cowboy hat had a broad brim that protected the cowboy from sun, rain, and snow. It also protected his eyes and head from low, thorny branches. A cowboy could drink water from his hat or use it to give water or food to his horse.

Boots

Boots were made of leather and designed so the heels and narrow toes fit well into the stirrups of a saddle.

Cowboys, Dangers, and Guns

Trail life was dangerous. **Stampedes** could knock a cowboy off his horse to his death; a longhorn could gore him; flash floods could drown him. More rarely, snakes, scorpions, grizzlies or mountain lions could end his life suddenly.

Yet the dangers that make great cowboy movies and stories exciting were rare. Although battles with Native Americans or rustlers were uncommon, cowboys did have guns, usually Colt pistols.

If a gun was shot, it was for practical and necessary reasons. Gunshots could be used as signals or to make stampeding cattle turn in a safer direction.

Cowboys shot plenty of threatening animals, but cowboys didn't always wear guns on the trail. Pistols were heavy, got in the way of roping and riding, and sometimes chafed a cowboy's body. On cattle drives, cowboys often left their guns in the chuck wagon.

The End of the Trail

In the 1880s, expansion broadened, and western territories filled with farmers and other settlers. Barbed wire crisscrossed open ranges and turned them into closed ranches.

Longhorns were replaced with new breeds of cattle that didn't travel as well. But cattle didn't have to travel well because trains reached more places, and soon long cattle drives were unnecessary.

The golden era of cowboys and cattle drives ended. It had lasted 30 years or so and involved about 30,000 real cowboys. But those hardy men made a lasting impression. Cowboy legends have survived and thrived ever since, and they always will.

Today tributes to The Old West are held annually in Sturgis, South Dakota. The photo below shows Sturgis's main street circa 1890.

Check In Why did the era of the cowboy on the trail come to an end?

GENRE Historical Fiction

Read to find out about a legend of the American West.

ANNIE OAKLEY

POSTERS AROUND THE COUNTRY HAILED ANNIE AS A DEADEYE "**SHARPSHOOTER** FROM THE FAR WEST." SHE WAS AN INCREDIBLY GOOD SHOT, BUT SHE GUARDED A DEEP SECRET.

FRANK WAS CELEBRATED AS A CRACK ***MARKSMAN***. YET ON A FATEFUL DAY, A SHOCKING SHOOTING CONTEST LED HIM TO LAY DOWN HIS GUNS FOREVER.

AND THE WILD WEST SHOW

BY DENNIS FERTIG · ILLUSTRATED BY FEDERICO PIATTI

THIS WILY OLD CAPTAIN WAS THE WILD WEST SHOW'S TOP MARKSMAN. NO ONE THOUGHT HE WOULD EVER LEAVE THE SHOW, THAT IS, UNTIL TRAGEDY STRUCK.

WILLIAM CODY PRODUCED A BREATHTAKING SPECTACLE THAT DEPICTED LEGENDARY MOMENTS OF THE REAL AMERICAN WEST. THE SHOW WAS **AUTHENTIC**—EXCEPT FOR THE MOST SUCCESSFUL PART.

FEW PEOPLE KNEW THAT A MYSTERY MAN WHO OPERATED IN THE SHADOWS COULD HAVE SUCH A LASTING EFFECT ON THE WILD WEST. WAS ALL THAT POWER A GOOD THING?

PHOEBE ANN MOSES WAS BORN IN 1860, THE FIFTH DAUGHTER IN A DARKE COUNTY, OHIO, PIONEER FAMILY. AS THEY WORKED THEIR SMALL FARM, THE MOSES FAMILY HAD BOTH FRUITFUL YEARS AND CHALLENGING ONES.
PHOEBE IS TOO FANCY OF A NAME FOR OUR SISTER.
LET'S JUST CALL THE BABY *ANNIE*.
ANNIE'S MOTHER AND SISTERS LABORED DAILY DOING THE DIFFICULT THINGS THAT PIONEER WOMEN ALWAYS DID.
WE'LL HAVE PLENTY OF BEETS FOR NOW AND FOR CANNING FOR WINTER.
IT IS SO, SO HARD DIGGING THE BEETS OUT OF THE HARD GROUND!
YOUNG ANNIE LABORED DAILY AS WELL, BUT PREFERRED DOING THINGS THAT PIONEER MEN DID, SUCH AS TRAPPING AND HUNTING.
LET'S HOPE THIS LITTLE CORNSTALK TRAP WILL CATCH US A BIG, FAT BIRD FOR COOKING.
A TURKEY DINNER WOULD BE SO MUCH BETTER THAN BEETS!
ANNIE WASN'T ALLOWED TO SHOOT LIKE THE MEN WERE, BUT THERE WAS A RUMOR THAT SHE BORROWED HER FATHER'S KENTUCKY LONG RIFLE WHEN SHE WAS JUST EIGHT YEARS OLD.
I JUST HOPE THAT WILD TURKEY DOESN'T DECIDE TO MOVE.
SHARP-EYED TEENAGER ANNIE HUNTED SMALL GAME—WILD TURKEY, QUAIL, AND RABBIT-AND SOLD THEM TO A LOCAL GENERAL STORE. FROM THOSE DAYS UNTIL SHE DIED MANY DECADES LATER, ANNIE CONTINUALLY EARNED HER LIVING WITH HER SHOOTING SKILLS.
WHERE DID THAT LITTLE GIRL GET SUCH A BASKETFUL OF FRESH GAME?
THAT LITTLE GIRL IS ANNIE MOSES, THE BEST SHOT IN DARKE COUNTY-AND MAYBE THE WHOLE WORLD.
OPEN
THIS YOUNG WOMAN MAY BE WORTH WATCHING.

IN THOSE DAYS, PEOPLE LOVED SHARPSHOOTING. SKILL WITH A RIFLE, SHOTGUN, OR SIX-SHOOTER WAS OFTEN A NECESSITY IN AMERICA'S WILDER TERRITORIES, AND IT WAS ADMIRED EVERYWHERE. CONTESTS AT SHOOTING **RANGES** DREW FAMOUS SHOOTERS AND LARGE AUDIENCES.
THAT MUST BE MR. FRANK BUTLER, THE FAMOUS SHARPSHOOTER.
BLAM
AMERICA'S BEST-KNOWN MARKSMEN WERE CAPTAIN ADAM H. BOGARDUS AND DOC CARVER. FRANK BUTLER WAS ALMOST AS FAMOUS AND ALMOST AS GOOD, OR SO HE THOUGHT.
I CAN OUTSHOOT ANYONE LIVING EXCEPT BOGARDUS OR CARVER.
WELL, MR. BUTLER, I WILL WAGER $100 THAT YOU CAN'T BEAT DARKE COUNTY'S CHAMPION SHOOTER.
THIS BUTLER IS PRETTY GOOD, BUT I HAVE A FEELING ABOUT YOUNG ANNIE MOSES.
WHEN FRANK BUTLER ACCEPTED THE WAGER, HE ASSUMED THAT THE DARKE COUNTY CHAMPION WOULD BE A MAN ABOUT HIS AGE AND WHO COULD EASILY BE BEATEN. WHEN HE DISCOVERED THAT THE COUNTY CHAMP WAS A YOUNG WOMAN, ANNIE MOSES, FRANK WAS STUNNED.
I AM VERY PLEASED TO MEET YOU, MISS MOSES.
AND I AM PLEASED, AS WELL. I HOPE WE WILL BE FRIENDS, NO MATTER WHAT.
FRANK BUTLER'S AMAZEMENT GREW CONSIDERABLY WHEN HE LOST THE SHOOTING MATCH TO THE YOUNG WOMAN.
CRASH
CRASH
BLAM
BLAM
I HIT 24 OUT OF 25 TARGETS, MISS MOSES.
YOU MISSED ONLY ONE, BUT I SHATTERED ALL 25 OF THEM, MR. BUTLER.
AS IMPRESSED AS FRANK WAS BY ANNIE'S SHOOTING, HE WAS EVEN MORE IMPRESSED BY HER PERSONALITY. FRANK WAS CHARMED AND FELL IN LOVE WITH THE YOUNG MARKSWOMAN. ANNIE SOON FELL IN LOVE WITH FRANK, AND THEY MARRIED IN 1876.
ANNIE AND FRANK'S MARRIAGE LASTED UNTIL THEIR DEATHS 50 YEARS LATER.

ANNIE OAKLEY
SHARPSHOOTER FROM THE FAR WEST
SELLS BROTHERS
CIRCUS & MENAGERIE
ANNIE USED THE STAGE NAME *ANNIE OAKLEY*, AND SHE AND FRANK STARTED A SHOOTING ACT TOGETHER CALLED "BUTLER & OAKLEY." WHILE PERFORMING IN THE SELLS BROTHERS CIRCUS, ANNIE WAS BILLED AS A "SHARPSHOOTER FROM THE FAR WEST."
MY SECRET IS THAT I NEVER LIVED IN THE WEST.
THE CROWDS WILL ALWAYS CHEER FOR YOU ANNIE NO MATTER WHERE YOU ARE FROM!
ANNIE AND FRANK REALLY HOPED TO JOIN BUFFALO BILL'S WILD WEST SHOW WHERE THEY KNEW ANNIE WOULD BE A REAL SHOOTING STAR. THEY HOPED THEY COULD GET BUFFALO BILL INTERESTED IN HER.
"DEAR MR. CODY,
I WRITE TODAY TO INFORM YOU ABOUT A REMARKABLY TALENTED YOUNG MARKSWOMAN . . ."

BUFFALO BILL CODY WAS BORN IN 1846, AND BECAME AN AUTHENTIC WESTERN HERO. DURING HIS LIFETIME, HE WAS A PONY EXPRESS RIDER,
. . . A UNION SOLDIER,
. . . A BUFFALO HUNTER,
. . . AND A SCOUT FOR THE U.S. CAVALRY. HE BATTLED AND LATER BEFRIENDED NATIVE AMERICANS.
IN THE 1880S, WHEN THE AMERICAN WEST WAS CHANGING, BUFFALO BILL DECIDED TO COMMEMORATE ITS SPIRIT WITH HIS WILD WEST SHOW. ACROSS AMERICA AND THE WORLD, MILLIONS OF PEOPLE WERE DAZZLED AS HIS TROUPE CELEBRATED THE EXCITING DAYS OF ADVENTURE IN OLD WEST TERRITORIES.
BUFFALO BILL STUDIED FRANK'S LETTER, CONSIDERED HIS REQUEST, AND FINALLY REJECTED IT. THE WILD WEST SHOW ALREADY HAD AMERICA'S TOP SHARPSHOOTING ACT FEATURING CAPTAIN BOGARDUS AND HIS FOUR SONS, AND BUFFALO BILL ALSO WORRIED THAT ANNIE WAS TOO FRAGILE TO HANDLE SHOTGUNS IN PERFORMANCES EVERY DAY.
"DEAR MR. BUTLER,
I AM IMPRESSED BY ANNIE OAKLEY'S GREAT SKILL BUT REGRET . . ."
BUFFALO BILL'S WILD WEST SHOW DELIGHTED WORLDWIDE AUDIENCES FOR 30 YEARS.

YET WITHIN WEEKS, TRAGEDY STRUCK AND THINGS CHANGED DRAMATICALLY. THE WILD WEST SHOW'S STEAMBOAT COLLIDED WITH ANOTHER BOAT AND SUNK IN THE MISSISSIPPI RIVER, SENDING MUCH OF THE SHOW'S EQUIPMENT, INCLUDING CAPTAIN BOGARDUS'S GUNS AND TARGETS, DEEP INTO THE MURKY WATERS.
NO GUNS AND NO EQUIPMENT MEANS I QUIT!
BUFFALO BILL NOW NEEDED A NEW SHARPSHOOTER ACT, SO HE RELUCTANTLY INVITED ANNIE TO LOUISVILLE FOR AN AUDITION.
I STILL DON'T KNOW IF SUCH A SMALL PERSON CAN HANDLE THOSE HEAVY SHOTGUNS.
THIS YOUNG ANNIE OAKLEY IS MUCH STRONGER THAN SHE LOOKS.
ANNIE AND FRANK TOOK A TRAIN TO CINCINNATI WHERE THEY COULD PRACTICE FOR SEVERAL WEEKS ON A FANCY TRAPSHOOTING RANGE.
213

TO PROVE THAT SHE WAS READY FOR THE WILD WEST SHOW AND WASN'T TOO FRAGILE TO HANDLE HEAVY SHOTGUNS, FRANK GAVE ANNIE A TOUGH TEST. FRANK USED THEIR SMALL TRAPSHOOTING MACHINES TO FLING GLASS BALLS HIGH INTO THE AIR. IN A ONE-DAY TEST, FRANK SENT 5,000 BALLS SKYWARD, AND ANNIE HIT 4,772 OF THEM.
NO ONE CAN OUTSHOOT THIS DAZZLING YOUNG SHARPSHOOTER!
AND FEW MEN CAN HANDLE A HEAVY SHOTGUN LIKE THAT SMALL, YOUNG WOMAN DOES.
523
BLAM
BLAM
CRASH
CRASH
UNBELIEVABLE! NEARLY ALL 5,000 HIT!
ANNIE'S TARGETS WERE GLASS BALLS FILLED WITH FEATHERS.
CRASH

WHEN THE BIG DAY IN LOUISVILLE FINALLY ARRIVED, ANNIE PRACTICED HER ACT ONCE MORE IN AN EMPTY BASEBALL PARK WHERE THE WILD WEST SHOW WOULD LATER PERFORM. FRANK SET UP TARGETS AND FLUNG BALLS INTO THE AIR, WHILE IN THE SHADOWS, MYSTERY MAN NATE SALSBURY SECRETLY OBSERVED.
ANNIE STARTED SLOWLY, SHOOTING AT ONE, TWO, THREE, AND THEN FOUR BALLS AT A TIME. SOON SHE WAS WHIRLING EVERY WHICH WAY, SHOOTING BALL AFTER BALL OUT OF THE SKY.
STARTING SLOWLY AND THEN BUILDING UP SPEED IS GOOD SHOWMANSHIP.
THEN ANNIE GRABBED TWO HANDGUNS AND FIRED RAPIDLY FIRST WITH HER RIGHT HAND AND THEN WITH HER LEFT, NEVER MISSING.
BANG BANG BANG
BANG BANG
SHE IS A PERFECT SHOT WITH EITHER HAND!
ANNIE MOVED QUICKLY AND GRACEFULLY, GRABBING OTHER LOADED AND READY SHOTGUNS. SHE RAPIDLY FIRED FROM OVER HER SHOULDER AND HIT HER TARGETS; SHE LAID ON HER BACK AND HIT HER TARGETS; SHE USED A MIRROR AND HIT HER TARGETS.
KRAK
BLAM
I KNEW SHE WAS GOOD, BUT SHE JUST CAN'T MISS!

ANNIE STOOD ON ONE SIDE OF A TABLE AND WAITED FOR A BALL TO SPIRAL INTO THE AIR.
SWOOOOOSH
THEN ANNIE LEAPED OVER THE TABLE,
. . . GRABBED A SHOTGUN,
. . . AND FIRED, EXPLODING THE TARGET IN MID-AIR.
CRASH
BLAM
ANNIE OAKLEY WILL BECOME THE GREATEST STAR IN THE WILD WEST SHOW TROUPE.
NATE SALSBURY, A WILD WEST SHOW TALENT SCOUT AND BUFFALO BILL'S BUSINESS PARTNER, HAD LONG BEEN THE SPY IN ANNIE'S LIFE. THAT MORNING IN LOUISVILLE, NATE HIRED ANNIE AND FRANK ON THE SPOT WITHOUT CHECKING WITH BUFFALO BILL.
ANNIE OAKLEY
BUFFALO BILL'S WILD WEST
ANNIE QUICKLY BECAME THE BIGGEST SUCCESS IN THE WILD WEST SHOW, EVEN THOUGH SHE HAD NEVER LIVED IN THE WEST!
Check In Why did Bill Cody change his mind about Annie Oakley?

Discuss Information

1. How do you think the three pieces in this book relate to the theme of *The Old West*?

2. How does the speaker's point of view affect the description of the setting in the song "Home on the Range"?

3. What information from "Cowboy History" was most interesting to you? Why?

4. Look at pp. 8 and 9 in "Cowboy History." What items protected cowboys from weather and other natural elements? How do they do that?

5. "Annie Oakley and the Wild West Show" is historical fiction that is based on real life. Look at the illustrations of clothing and gear. How are they similar to the authentic cowboy gear shown in "Cowboy History"?

6. What do you still want to learn about The Old West? What questions do you have about the time period and the people?